DIY Survival Projects:
Survival Ideas For Getting Food and Water, Self Protection And Other Basic Needs

Table of Contents

Introduction

Welcome to DIY Projects for Survival, a DIY book designed to help you assess what you need to take care of immediately. This book is about recognizing the situation that you are in, distinguishing what you want from what you need, and the find the tools around you to get what you need. Let's begin.

Chapter 1 – Basic Needs Assessment

In all situations that require survival for any period of time you will need to assess what you *need*. Not what you *want*, but what you need. There is a big difference between want and need, which is why the first chapter will be dedicated to help you identify needs. There are five primary *needs* that you will need to keep an eye on in order to survive any given situation.

Injuries and Infections

If you are **put** into a survival situation, as this book is made for, then your primary concern is any person that is injured or has an infection. You can drink all the water you want and eat all the food you want for days, but that doesn't stop your body parts from rotting off your body. Injuries are the quickest ways to die in a survival situation, which is why it is almost always the primary need for any survival assessment.

How do you assess an Injury or Infection?

I am no doctor by any means and you should confirm everything I type with a doctor, but diagnosing a general injury or infection is relatively easy. There are a few colors that take place that you need to pay attention to and they go in this order: Red, Blue, White, Purple, and Black.

Red means that the location is currently irritated, which also usually means that the immune system is fighting with whatever happens to be trying to get inside. Blue means that the area is full of blood, which can either mean you've punctured an important part or the area has begun to lack oxygen. White usually represents "frothing", which is a way to say that the area is full of bacteria. White is the good part that you see when you use something like Hydrogen Peroxide because it is killing the bacteria. Purple represents two things, depending on location of the color. If there is no breakage of skin, purple represents the *build up* of blood *and* the damaging of inner muscles. Bruises are a great example of this, but if there has been no outside injury then it means that limb is at risk for a blood clot. If there is a breakage of skin and the purple is on the top layer, where the broken skin is, then that means that skin has begun to die. If the purple is on the muscle, the muscle has begun to die. Black is death and it means those cells will continue to kill the cells that it is connected to.

Water

Water is the item most people go to when they think of the primary *need* and, for the most part, it is true. However, how do you assess if you need water or not? This has to do with how long you have been without water. Normally, you want to get water within the very first day if not the second day and you will die in the third day unless you are one of those individuals who is lucky enough not to be a statistic.

Infection

Once again, we come back to the very first *need* that I mentioned before because the water you find is useless if there are too many parasites, chemicals, and bacteria in it. Infections from the water will often leave you more dehydrated than when you drank the water in the first place. The standard way to remove parasites and bacteria so that they cannot infect you is to bring the water to a boiling point, filter it in some way, and then bring it back up to boiling point. The first boiling kills all the easy ones and filtering removes those. The second boiling kills all the difficult ones. You can filter again, but since they are most likely dead they will pass right through your system.

Shelter

The third need coincides with the fourth need, but this *need* also protects you from things like mudslides, tornadoes, and similar natural disaster. Shelter will be the only one we don't cover here, primarily because there are so many different types of shelters you need based on a situation that you simply can't cover it in a short novel.

Cold or Warmth

Your body needs to be kept at a specific temperature: 98.6 degrees give or take a few degrees. This is your fourth need when it comes to survival and while it may be easy to know how to keep it at that area, it is often difficult to implement that know how. However, how do you assess that you need a different temperature and what will that assessment lead to? **Are you comfortable?** Ironically, this is the only need that follows your comfort level. When you are comfortable with the temperature, you are at the right temperature to stabilize your body's temperature. If you are too hot, this is usually caused by the sun so get out of direct impact of the sun and try to keep hydrated if there is nothing cold near you. If you are too cold, this is normally caused by the wind so get out of the wind and cover up/huddle with the nearest friendly warm body.

If you are wet, you can become too cold or too hot depending on the situation, but you are likely to become too cold. If you are wet outside of a body of water then you need to dry off immediately while heading towards a place of shelter. If you are **safe** inside a body of water and only feel the temperature difference outside of the water, then find a shelter close enough to the body of water where you can get out and run to the shelter. Even though you are okay most of the time underneath that water, some water is so cold that you cannot feel it but there's too much of the water for it to full freeze. An example of this is a frozen lake, which will usually only have the top layer frozen.

Food

Food is the last *need* and, once again, this comes down to whether you need it or not rather than whether your stomach is causing you massive amounts of pain. Going any longer three weeks is a bad idea, but you can generally survive a long time without the need of food inside of you. Sadly, many people find that they think it is their second or third need, when you can, in fact, survive the longest without it.

Infection

The standard way to remove parasites and bacteria so that they cannot infect you is to bring the water to a boiling point, filter it in some way, and then bring it back up to boiling point. The first boiling kills all the easy ones and filtering removes those. The second boiling kills all the difficult ones. You can filter again, but since they are most likely dead they will pass right through your system.

Protection

Oddly enough, this one is in limbo because you do need to protect yourself but, sometimes, you need to not protect yourself in order to survive. For example, you are up against a group of people that are protecting themselves but they have food, water, and shelter. Unless they're psychotic, they have very little reason to kill you beyond being a potential threat. By not protecting yourself aka announcing you are not looking for a fight and lowering your weapon, you have a slim chance of being accepted and getting easy access to those resources. On the other hand, you need to protect yourself against the wild animals that will undoubtedly show up in the streets.

Welcome to the end of this Chapter, where we went over your primary needs in a survival situation. We will also go over DIY projects that help and support those needs in the coming chapters. The point of this guide is to help your survival, but we cannot guarantee it. It is entirely up to you to ensure your survival in a given situation so make sure you expand your knowledge before such a situation happens so you have a better chance at surviving.

Chapter 2 – Water

To make clean water is actually not that difficult but it is also circumstantial. I will show you the most basic method there is and then the most preferred.

Basic Water Filtration

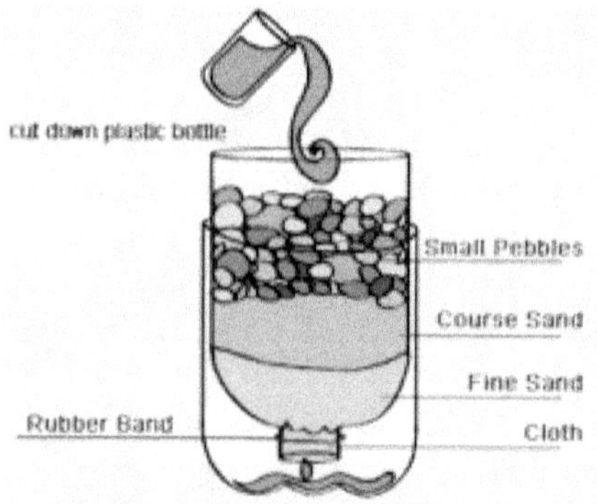

All you need is the environment around you, something sharp, and a bottle. Use the sharp item that you have to cut the bottle in half horizontally with the bottle facing upright. Then, go to your body of water, which is likely going to be a river, and find the shallow portion of the water. Here you will find the three items you need: small rocks, rough sand, and fine sand. Take your shirt off and place it on the ground. The first layer you want to have on the shirt is fine sand. Then you want rough sand with the rocks on top. Bring all four corners to the middle so that you can lift this layered ground *off* the ground and then place it in the portion of the bottle that has a nozzle. Finally, place the nozzle over the other half portion of the bottle and pour water over the filtration system you just made. By being the most basic, it also means that it is not perfect. Additionally, I suggest you run the water through multiple times to filter it even more. Even though you can technically drink it after the first time, this method is not perfect in removing everything and doing it more than once lowers the chances.

Advanced Water Filtration

The best way to filtrate water beyond having some commercially made item is to collect steam. The way you do this is you boil one container while having a hose connected to collect that steam and transfer it into another container. When you boil water into steam, you are transforming that water into a system of gas. Parasites and Diseases cannot live in most forms of gas, especially parasites as they are made up of heavy bodies that cannot be transported by gas. The steam is, therefore, cleansed of nearly all of the issues by its lonesome, but you have to boil water in order to create steam. This kills anything even if that thing is transferred over to the other bottle. Beyond commercial methods, this is the most advanced water filtration system that you can have using random materials.

Chapter 3 – Cold and Warmth

Welcome to the Cold and Warmth section, which is a section dedicated to either protecting you from the cold or the heat. Each one of these D.I.Y. projects will be situational most of the time, which means that you will only be able to do them in an emergency. For instance, the Brick Rocket Stove is only when there is an abandoned Lowes or something similar around or there is a lot of brick rubble. If you're out in the wilderness, you will not *likely* be able to build a Brick Rocket Stove. So, let's begin our first project, the basic fire.

Basic Fire

A basic fire is really easy to make, if you know how to make it. You just need something to light on fire and something that produces fire. The problem comes in what you use to produce the fire because as an arsonist can tell you, you can almost always set something on fire somewhere. The obvious choice is the lighter, which can be picked up from an abandoned gas station or nearly any abandoned commercial store nowadays.

The second choice is to grab a bunch of long weeds, a medium straight stick, a sharp rock, two wide pieces of wood and a small straight stick. Take the sharp rock and cut notches into the medium straight stick near the ends of each side. Bend the stick as much as you can without it breaking and then tie the weeds to the stick to hold the position of the bent stick. Finally, place the small straight stick in the middle of the weeds and flip the bent stick over to trap the small straight stick in the middle. This will be your fire starter, but you need to take it so at first. You place the small straight stick on one of the wide pieces of wood and then place the other wide piece of wood on the other end of the small straight stick, which you will hold down as hard as you can. Very slowly, you can begin to push and pull on the bent stick to turn the small straight stick. You do not want to go fast at first because you risk breaking it. You will eventually be able to get up to the proper speed to create a small flicker of smoke on the bottom piece. You will then blow on this until you see a small flame, which you can then put something dry on so that the dry material lights on fire and you can build a more substantial fire out of it.

Brick Rocket Stove

The Brick Rocket Stove is basically a mini-chimney, but you will need at least twenty-four bricks in order to make one and you will need something made of metal that has a lot of holes in it. One of those bricks will have to broken in half across the middle the short way in order for this to work properly.

First layer

Lay two blocks parallel to each other. Above them (not on top of them) lay one half and a block. Push the previous two blocks apart until their outside parameters match those of the ones above it. Place the piece of metal over the open area that should have been created by doing this.

Second layer and Beyond

The second layer will be identical to the first so that you can trap the metal in between the two layers. Once you have these layers done, you can make the third layer, which will repeat itself in every layer afterwards. You just need to place each brick perpendicular to the last one with their outside perimeters lining up. After this, it just repeats itself into a chimney.

How to Use It and How it Works

Now, the top part of the metal is where you will place the wood for the fire. Most would logically conclude that the bottom would be where the fire goes, but the holes in the metal are supposed to allow air through them. The big hole that feeds into the fire makes an air tunnel that leads into the hole and focuses the heat into the chimney. Once the fire has been started, you can then see this in action as the flame will climb up to the top of the stove.

Egg Carton Fire Starter

For this you will need an empty egg carton and some Crisco, or some other type of fatty oil. You rip the top off of this egg carton and split it into pieces that will fit into each pocket evenly. Put a spoon full of Crisco in each pocket and the cover each pocket with the pieces from the top of the egg carton. What this will do is light the pieces on fire and then the fat will keep the fire from going out for a rather lengthy bit of time. Now, if you want to prep this beforehand then you also have the option of heating up the fat so that you can pour it in. This allows you to occupy a lot of the space inside without wasting room, which means that the firestarter will last for much longer than if you were to just use a spoonful of Crisco. However, I prefer to give you the option of knowing both so you can make one before and after a situation.

Solar Cooker

For this, you will need a box, a pot, and some aluminum foil. Just to be clear, there are more solar efficient options out there but this is the bare minimum. You want to cover the inside of the box in aluminum foil and spread the flaps out so that they collect a lot of sun but are still redirecting light into the box. Put your pot in with water ever you want to cook and watch it cook. Normally we are heated up by the sun as it is but not on a level that cooks us. When you redirect several layers of the sun into one area, the temperature in that area rises very quickly and because heat cannot travel at the speed of light we create a bubble of heat that's very intense. The metal is both reflective enough to do this and will also retain the heat as it heats up very quickly. This is how a solar cooker works.

Chapter 4 – Food

Welcome to the Food section, which is an area of this book that will not be going over DIY Food projects but rather how to cook your food properly. We will also be going over how to vacuum seal your food without a machine and how to dehydrate your meat when you have no machine. Vacuum sealing and dehydration are both methods you can use to extend how long you will be able to eat meat. This is standard prepper knowledge, but it is also useful to know how to do this after you are in a survival situation.

Cooking Your Meat: Beef and Pork

Slabs of red meat are often the easiest to cook if you have gotten a hold of them fresh. You can cut them from a dead body easily and you can cook them easily, but, just as easily, they could be infected with parasites. Therefore, red meat is something you don't really want to rely on when you are looking for meat unless you have to.

Unlike what most people tell you, the optimum way to cook beef is not to cook it over an open fire. Unless cooked until beyond well done, you will likely not kill all of the parasites inside of the red meat. Instead, the optimum way to cook beef to make sure that it is safe is to boil it. By boiling it, you raise the fluid temperature of the entire piece of meat, which means that you raise the temperature of all the nooks and crannies the parasites ate through. By cooking the meat on the outside, the heat won't be sufficient enough to kill almost all the parasites until the outside of the meat is practically inedible because it is a meat wood chip.

The reason why to cooking method is still used is because the **odds** of something happening are **significantly lower** due to the fact that you kill a general portion of them. Remember that the parasites must survive your stomach acid and they don't actually survive, but reproduce enough or bury themselves far enough into the food that the stomach acid can't kill all of them. It only takes one of those little suckers to survive the acid bath, which is why most survivalists cook in small scraps but don't tell you or are not informed that, by doing so, this lowers the likelihood of the survival of that one parasite. Since the mathematical odds have been lowered so much, you only get fringe cases of this not working.

How do you know your Red Meat is done?

It'll be brown and tough. You could also use the hand to figure it out, but it's easier just to cook it all the way through then open it up to look at the inside. I'm not going to give out the "steak" advice, which is the hand technique I gave you before because with Red Meat you do not **want** raw of any kind lest you be infected by something you didn't kill.

Cooking Your Meat: Bird

DO NOT KILL AND EAT BIRDS. I am extremely serious about this. Unless you have the professional tools to skin, cook, and prepare a bird, do not try to kill these. Not only are they notoriously difficult to kill all by your lonesome without a gun, but they are riddled with diseases and parasites. Since species of bird (and other flying beings) are able to carry diseases and parasites, most species of diseases and parasites are specifically designed not to kill the bird they are in for a long time. Winged creatures are the fastest way to spread beyond wind, so evolution in parasites has adopted into not killing the winged creature on most occasions.

You might think this is odd because *evolution doesn't have a memory*. However, evolution kind of does: the memory of the fittest. Only the genes of those who survive pass on in the world, so if you follow the logical path of best survival then you will see that parasites that travelled in the air survived the most. Instead of growing wings, the evolution focuses around being better at infecting the targets that these winged creatures focus on, which ironically brings us to the meat that you should rely on the most.

Cooking Your Meat: Fish

Specifically, large fish. You do not want to go after anything that's smaller than your hand for a few reasons.

- The smaller the fish, the deadlier they are. Small fish will eat things like parasites and other bacterial-sized creatures because that is what is available for them and that is what works.

- These types of fish are often the target of nearly every class of bird. The larger the fish you hunt for, the less competition you have to deal with.

You also don't want to go after any massively large fish because of mercury. The larger the fish, the longer they tend to live, the more mercury they tend to accumulate. For instance, your common store salmon can be eaten for up to 18 ounces a week but something like a Grouper is something you just don't want to

The best part about how to tell if a fish is cooked is really simple, you just:

- Take a Fork-like object

- Poke it in at an angle

- Push upwards

- See if it flakes apart like a hard cookie

That's right, it is that simple. Fish meat is flaky once fully cooked and also white. If it isn't fully cooked then it will resist and the opacity of the fish will be like a murky water.

Chapter 5 – Protection

Protection is really easy, but the way people tend to describe how to make sure weapons pertain to mostly forest or wooded survival. Therefore, when I type in the projects they will be generalized rather than specific. This helps you see objects around you as something that can be transformed into a weapon. Let's do this.

Spear

The spear is often the easiest to make because all you need is a long pole, a small sharp object, and something to wrap the sharp object to the long pole. You would think that the goal is to wrap the sharp object to the long pole, but that is only partially true. If you were to make your spear like this then the sharp object would break off either before it entered the body or afterwards. The way you prevent this is with the last object you need (glue) and the step that was forgotten. Instead of just tying it to the spear, you need to use the sharp object to cut a notch on the end so that the sharp object can sit in it. Then you can apply glue (in the wild this would be sap) and then wrap the sharp object up. Now what will happen is that the glue and wrapping will put resistance on the sharp object to prevent it from turning.

Hammer

The hammer is a little bit different, but has a very similar process. Instead of a sharp object, you need a large blunt round object and you will likely need a much wider base on your pole while also having it short enough to be carried in the hand. There are two ways you can do this. If you can split the top part in half, then you can place the blunt object in between. This will allow you to secure it into place by wrapping the whole thing up. If you cannot, then you will have to choose one side and tie the large blunt object to it. The reason why you want to be able to do the first one is that is makes the hammer much harder to "break" and by break I mean the wrapping comes loose so that the large object falls out.

Knife

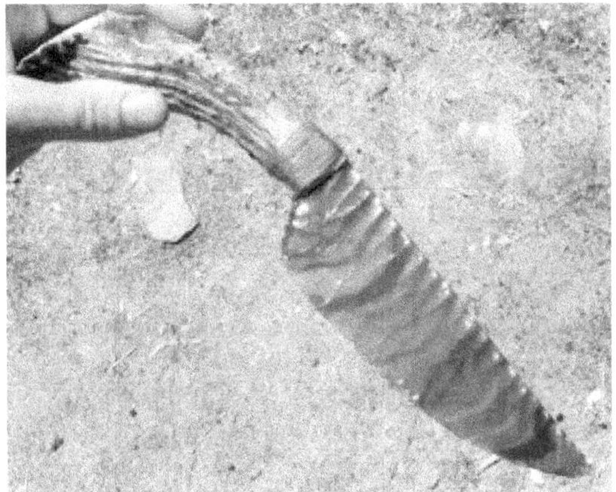

The knife is a shorter version of the spear with a longer tip. Normally, you find something that can be used as a knife already. If you are dealing with a rock, you can generally just slam it into another rock to get a knife like rock. Then you find a large stick that you can embed a small portion of the bladed object into. Finally, you wrap up the entire handle so that you don't cut yourself when you go use it on something.

Those were the survival weapons you can build in, generally, nearly every survival situation you may happen to be able to contend with. After all, you may be able to build a spear but a tornado will pick you up just the same whereas a knife might be able to prevent yourself from being trapped under water in a mudslide.

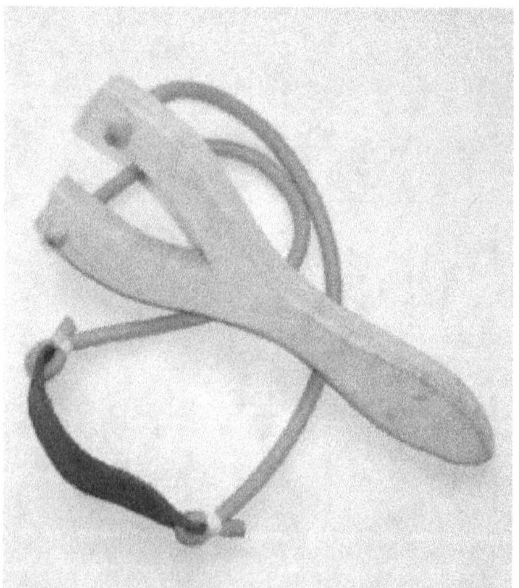

This one is a little bit different than the others because you have to be in a city and you have to have access to either rubber bands or security straps made of rubber. A lot of people think that you just need a single line of bouncy rubber and something to shoot, but this is only if you want to gamble with your shots. Instead, you want two layers of rubber and then you also want a second set around a half inch to an inch below or above that. Keep in mind that you do not need two rows that are separate, but it certainly helps and adds more resistance, which means that your shot will hit harder the more you can pull it back. Obviously, you will also need an item that is Y-shaped with a lot of resistance. The thicker the rubber is, the more deadly the shot will be. Additionally, you want a small bit of cloth to go in the middle so that you can put something like a rock in there. To make the slingshot more deadly, go with something like a jax but make sure you sharpen the edges. Just to be clear, this will likely not kill anything beyond on bird but it will certainly make wild animals think twice about attacking you when they know you can inflict damage from afar.

Torch

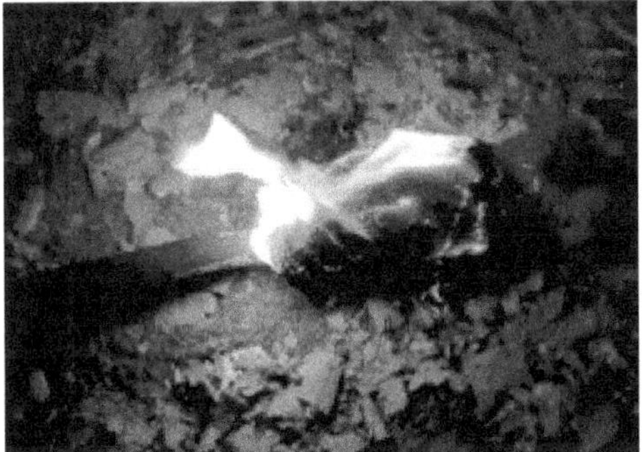

You will need some liquid that is flammable but the liquid needs to be thick. You will also need a rag and a stick. Wrap the rag around the top of the stick, dunk it into the liquid, wrap the rag around some more, and repeat the process until there is no more rag. A torch is a great tool to see at night but it is also a great weapon if you need to use it as a weapon. Just remember that an animal doesn't know what fire is so if it moves around quickly and hurts, it will usually deter most predators through intimidation. Do not use gas and try to go with oils.

Conclusion

Welcome to the end of this book and we've covered a lot in here. However, this is just a representative into the rest of this subject as there are a lot more ways you can build items to help you survive. Until next time, good luck.

OR Go to this URL

http://zbit.ly/1WBb1Ek